Mississippi Meanderings

poems by

Barb Geiger

Finishing Line Press
Georgetown, Kentucky

Mississippi Meanderings

ACKNOWLEDGMENTS

I'm grateful to Kathie Giorgio and my talented colleagues at AllWriters'
Workplace & Workshop for their inspiration and encouragement during
my writing journey. I've also learned much from the fine examples of poets
Jim Landwehr, Kathrine Yets, Margaret Rozga, Cristina Norcross, and many
others whose work I admire.

The ideas for poems in this collection had their seeds in the lives and stories
of residents, travelers, and wildlife along the Mississippi River and Tenn-Tom
Waterway. I'm thankful for each of their stories and to God, Creator of the
beautiful ecosystem we grew to love.

Finally, I'd like to express my gratitude to Leah and the staff at Finishing Line
Press for believing in me and publishing my work, and to the many kind
readers who welcome my musings into their minds and hearts. Thank you all.

Publisher: Leah Huete de Maines
Editor: Christen Kincaid
Cover Art: Barb Geiger
Author Photo: Mortensen Studio
Cover Design: Elizabeth Maines McCleavy

Order online: www.finishinglinepress.com
also available on amazon.com

Author inquiries and mail orders:
Finishing Line Press
PO Box 1626
Georgetown, Kentucky 40324
USA

Contents

Dedicated to my husband, Gene,
whose grand dreams fill my life with adventure,
and whose love and encouragement
support those of my own.

Photo by Constancia Roling

Preface

Shortly after my retirement, my husband and I slipped the tandem wooden kayak we built into the headwaters of the Mississippi River, embarking on a five-month journey to the sea. Along the way, we paused in quaint river towns to volunteer with non-profit organizations and blog about their missions. Our experiences on the river and the amazing people we met inspired my memoir, *Paddle for a Purpose*, and instilled in me a lasting love for this iconic waterway, a magnificent gem in the heartland of our country.

The poems in this collection invite you to leisurely meander along with us, experiencing the Mississippi, Tennessee and Tombigbee Rivers through lyrical snapshots along the way. Photos accompanying the poems can be found on my author website, *www.barbgeiger.com*. Simply scan the QR code below if you'd like to view the pictures as you read. For follow-up activities, you'll also find a free discussion guide, including background information, discussion questions and writing prompts. Come along! Enjoy the journey!

Heartwaters
Dedicated to Anishinabe Artist, Jeff Savage

Children totter over mossy stones.
Clear sparkling water trickles between their toes,
swirls around grown-up ankles below rolled-up jeans.
Soft voices speak in hushed reverence
for the birthplace of the Mississippi.

Anishinabe woman, born of tradition and bronze,
hair flowing in waves like the river she protects,
keeps watch over the heartwaters of our nation.
Infant stream gathers strength, ripples past pine forests,
meanders through the land of her people.

Caretaker Woman leans over hatchling turtles
released from a basket still cradled in her arms.
Heads point to Grandfather Sun, tails toward Mother Earth.
Voiceless turtles speak for our water, land and air,
inspiring us to do the same.

Lesson from the Bogs

Miles of crystal stream wander idly
among floating bogs of bulrushes
and cattails clothed with velvet
seed pods, still young.

Wiggle-waggle switchbacks
branch into bewildering paths.
Reed heads waver in fickle breeze.
Surface ripples offer only indecision.

The headwaters whisper, "Look deeper."

Rooted below in riverbed silt,
supple fronds of elodea sway
seductively in siren dance,
tempt us toward their wayward path.

But 'round a bend, their serious siblings
lie prostrate, pushed to submission
by the channel's tenacious current,
ushering us toward the sea.

Banjo Man
Tribute to Gospel Folk Singer, Mike Turner

Melancholy strains drift among silent pines.
"The folk singer sings about life, about love.
The folk singer sings from his heart."

Tangerine sky swirls gold, fades denim blue.
Cascading spillway splashes in harmony.
"Run, run, Mississippi, run.
Run on down to the land of the sun."

Freshly-cut planks over glowing embers
crackle with ostinato rhythm.
"You're more than just a river, more than waters grand,
more than man can reason, God's wonder in our land."

Glowing embers fade to hills of dusty ash.
River and troubadour move on, soothing souls,
spreading word of God's majesty and love.

Riverside Seat

If I had a chair by the river,
nothing would ever get done.
I'd while away my idle days
watching turtles bask in the sun.

Weeds would take over the garden,
grass grow as tall as bamboo,
while I'd catch up on my reading
and pen a poem or two.

I'd barely note dishes pile up in the sink,
dust bunnies blow 'cross the floor.
Mesmerized from dawn 'til dusk,
as tranquility drifts alongshore.

It's best my backyard's not near water,
as much as I'd love it to be.
I can finish my chores, then recline in the shade,
watching clouds sail by in the breeze.

Stump Field Fishing

Curved talons grip gnarly roots,
arched in tangles above surface ripples.
Muscular wings rise, spread for balance,
reveal baggy feathered shorts,
legs surprisingly sturdy and tall.

Pacing along its makeshift pier,
predatory stares through river's glare
turn to wary sidelong glances.
Tandem kayakers drift near,
paddles suspended in hushed awe.

Secret spot no longer its own,
eagle angler launches in silent flight,
wings extended, feet tucked,
skirting the dappled shallows
in search of solitude.

Everyday Oatmeal

Packing oatmeal
for breakfast
six days a week,
with only
CoCo Wheats
for variety
seems wise
after months
spent dehydrating,
combining and
vacuum sealing
twenty weeks of
one-pot meals.

On the river,
appreciation for
a warm, filling
bellyful of
carb-loaded energy
to paddle for hours
devolves into
a quest
for variety:
added cinnamon,
raisins, almonds,
walnuts, dates…
anything edible.

We soon learn
oats are not
easily passed off
as hostess gifts
to those who
gladly offer us
their help
and homes,
but do make

a welcome treat
for ducks,
catfish,
and wily raccoons.

Pig's Eye Heron Rookery

Silent sentinel stands watch
among wind-blown cattails,
seed heads not yet formed.
Stick legs still, neck stretched taut,
hidden, but for wispy bib feathers
and golden Mona Lisa eyes.

I find it curious, this peaceful place
named for a bootlegging fur trader
who happened to put down roots,
build a still in a cave, sell hooch
to residents indigenous to this land,
to recent settlers and soldiers alike.

Distant, a towering leafless tree,
silvered with wind and time,
hosts a flock of great blues.
Extended wings, as if to take flight,
fold anew, balance regained.
Graceful ballet to nature's inaudible beat.

Small-scale cousins perch nearby,
atop tilted trunks near water's edge.
Black-crowned night herons
hunch over bellies of purest white,
waiting for wind to abate,
for us to paddle on.

Transient Home

Ripples trace our hull, vanish astern,
leave no hint of our fleeting presence.
Cradled in Mother Nature's arms,
we surrender to the river's will,
like the lazy russet leaves floating by.

Whitetails peek from aspen groves.
Stick-legged heron statues
follow us only with wary eyes.
New neighbors? Or trespassers
crossing their backyard?

Bald eagle escorts launch,
spread mighty wings, soar overhead.
We pause, watch, whisper our gratitude.
Someday, our paddles will reach the sea.
Until then, this river is our home.

Locking Through

Metal gates clank closed, our tiny craft floats alone
in the mammoth cavern designed with barges in mind.
Towering concrete walls obscure all but sky,
diminished to a rectangular patch of blue.

Somewhere deep below a valve opens,
drains our super-sized tub, baring water-dyed walls.
Damp line slides through my fingers, inch by inch.
Foot by foot, we descend further into darkness.

My body shudders in the chilly shadow of our confines.
I've never been in prison, but today it crosses my mind.
I count hash marks down the wall as we drop,
glance back and secretly hope the gates hold fast.

Ahead, massive doors creak open, an air horn blares
an unnecessary nudge into our new river pool,
where warm sunshine reflects an emerald shore,
and gossamer clouds drift across an endless azure sky.

Summer Storm

Restless geese patrol stump-field sand bars,
squawks overlapping with plaintive seagull cries.
Pregnant clouds darken the sky,
ominous, heavy and grey.

Frenzied anglers reel in untouched lines,
motors roar to life, bows point toward shore.
"Storm's comin'! Better head in!"
Someone shouts what everyone knows.

Picnic shelter tabletops offer front-row seats
to nature's show of power and might.
Raindrops pelt the surface of dimpled waves
churned up by howling winds.

Electrified air crackles, snaps.
Jagged lines of light carve
through a darkened daytime sky.
Moments later, Earth rumbles in reply.

Deluge turns to drizzle, rivulets slow to a trickle,
leaving riverbed patterns in campground soil,
rosy glow of early summer evening,
fresh smell of renewal.

Pelican Problem

Designed to float, pelicans paddle and bob,
pterodactyl heads held contentedly aloft,
casting for dinner with nature's nets.

Designed to soar, they circle above,
Blue Angel formations of ink-tipped wings,
aeronautic precision in graceful flight.

The pelican problem (as the kayaker) lies in transition:
waddle-run   (wiggle-step)
wing flap   (arm swing)
foot splash   (plop down)
lift off   (paddle on)

And always, pretend it was easy.

Sand Island Sunset

River shallows seep across
evening-darkened sand,
lacy ribbons of molten gold.

Silhouette barge vanishes downstream.
Its engine hum lingers, then disappears,
leaving only silence.

The world waits, holds its breath,
while a kaleidoscope sky glows,
whirls, dances, dims, then sighs.

Creation's lightshow ends
with moonlit indigo sky
and grateful heart.

Barge Race

With low resonant hum,
the titan rounds a river bend.
Spellbound, we do nothing
but evacuate its path,
settle in for the show.

Barges, four rows of three,
each seventy times our size,
maneuver steadily downstream,
towboat captain supervising
from wheelhouse above.

"You up for a race?" Gene asks.

Paddles churn, abs crunch, matching speed,
for a moment in time, with a Mississippi legend.
Conceding to its stamina and power,
we wave good-bye, with noodled arms,
to the unfazed behemoth leaving us in its wake.

Pearl Buttons

Tribute to John Boepple, Craftsman

From Germany he comes, in Iowa he settles,
button-making skills and tools his luggage,
intention and hope his companions.

By the river in Muscatine, a business is born,
crafting lustrous pearl buttons from nature,
freshwater mussels, plentiful and free.

Her iridescence embraced by the world,
Mississippi makes space along her banks
for new businesses, more profit, more fame.

Until, exhausted, she has no more to give.

From factory he closes, to hatchery he moves,
reversing damage he never intended to cause,
restoring the freshwater mussel to its Mississippi home.

River Addresses

"How can I locate your home
from the water, when paddling my 'yak?
Your street address isn't helpful at all.
The river's way out in the back."

"I live at Mile one twenty-five.
I'd love you to stop, if you will.
The house isn't easy to see through the trees,
just watch for the swing on the hill."

"Our home is near Mile four thirty-nine.
There's a lighthouse out on the rock.
If you find yourself in our neighborhood,
feel free to tie up at the dock."

"I live at Mile eight sixty-three.
However, to tell you the truth,
it's just as easy to keep an eye out
for the bright red telephone booth."

"A telephone booth? What a whimsical thought!
Finding your house won't be hard.
And…if you ever need Superman,
Clark can change right there in your yard."

Resilience

When spring rains swell the river, churned to chocolate brown,
and flotsam clutches trunks of wading island trees,
River folk shake their heads and say, "She's runnin' fast today."

If the river washes over its banks, fans out into delta,
and wind sloshes waves over the wooden plank pier,
River folk decide, "Best wait'n take the boat out tomorrow."

When submerged danger signs leave their warnings untold,
spillway gates are open, and the roar's too loud to speak,
River folk watch and shout, "Wouldn't want to be out there now!"

If the river creeps up their stairs, flows over the threshold,
trespasses through home or business, strips away all they own,
River folk rebuild.

Posting high-water marks on buildings as tribute,
Hanging photos of great floods on rebuilt walls,
River folk celebrate resilience, daring the river to do it again.

River Rat

"If you're on the river long enough,
you'll be a river rat, too." —Jason Marchand, Bemidji

Damp shoes, soaked socks,
uncut hair, tamed into a pony
tumbling out from brimmed cap.
Drops of rain from foggy spectacles
trace my life vest, faded to dull pink.

Who *is* this woman?

I hardly recognize my reflection
in the calm waters of the Mississippi,
steering our kayak toward the pebbled beach.
Bronze shoulders and paddle glove hands
pull pasty white legs from beneath the deck.

Minimal makeup long past moot,
polish chipped and scratched,
all pretense fallen away
like sculptor's scraps littering the floor,
uncovering the strong woman within.

And yet, this strong woman still shrieks with joy
to discover a hot shower and clean, ceramic loo.

Craft Envy

We hear the deep-throated hum
of twin inboard four-eighties,
turn our kayak into its wake,
ride the waves 'til they pass.
"She's a beauty," my husband says,
his eyes lingering on her stern.

Bayliner ski boat blasts past.
Tubers behind scream with glee.
We paddle to the lock,
find them swimming in wait.
"Sure looks fun!" I wave and shout,
sweat streaming down my back.

A woman leans over the gunwale
of her Grand Banks trawler,
offers fresh chocolate chip cookies
baked in the galley oven below deck.
"Thank you; you're so kind." I twist
in my cramped confines to offer a smile.

We nestle up to the marina pier,
between luxury craft umpteen times our size,
wander the docks, perusing boats for sale.
The captain of a nearby yacht calls over.
"That's a beautiful kayak. Did you build it?
I've always wanted to do that."

Inadequacies of our tiny craft vanish.
"Thanks, we sure did," I proudly reply.
Gene glances at the gleaming chrome
and glass of the captain's floating palace
and adds, "If you really like it,
we might be able to work out a trade."

Mississippi Melting Pot

Waking from winter slumber,
snowdrifts and ice crystals thaw,
drip into swollen creeks,
pour into your open arms.

Rainfall nourishes northern forests,
mid-west fields, wind-swept plains,
flows down mountainside streams
from Appalachia to Pikes Peak.

You welcome diverse origin,
color and composition to join you,
flow and dance by your side,
mix together until all become one.

And you find yourself
stronger than before.

Solitude

Still waters meet
sun-soaked sand, curve
with grace, like the neck
of an egret, whose elegant
wings spread as it lights
with the slightest
splash of
imagined
sound, content
to wade in shared
reflection with a
silent world.

Moonshine Jell-O Shots

We hear the Labor Day hoopla
before the calls of sun-kissed bodies,
swimming, laughing, waving us in.

Maybe just a short break to stretch our legs.
We slip our kayak onto the sand island shore
between ski boats, cruisers and yachts.

Minutes of partying stretch into hours
with strangers who feel like friends
after a few cool, fruity moonshine Jell-O shots.

Revelers head home with their boats, beer, and sunburns
while we set up camp to the fading hum of engines
before an evening stroll on our now private beach.

Brush Creek Belle
Tribute to Stan and Milton Cornelius

Shared dream of brothers long past grown,
set into motion with aging craigslist find.
Pontoon boat revitalized with thrift shop buys,
repurposed parts, rediscovered gear stored years ago.

Product of two-by-fours, plywood and PVC,
secured with nails, screws and loops of line,
ingenuity covered in blue tarpaulin blinds
and matching hand-lettered signs.

Brush Creek Belle and two brothers, young at heart,
drift past islands and Mississippi River towns,
bring awe and intrigue to those they meet,
offer courage to dream, "What if?"

Kentucky Lake Legacy
Tribute to residents of Danville, TN

What legacy remains of a town destroyed?
Families evicted, church doors closed,
buildings razed, streets and landmarks flooded,
history buried beneath water dammed.

Too expensive to destroy, too strong to fall,
graffiti-tagged towers of an old grain elevator
rise from the lake like an island oddity,
sentinel over hometown submerged.

Catfish forage among concrete pillars
where riverside barges met trackside trains,
swapped loads of peanuts and cotton,
oak barrel staves and distilled corn.

Anglers cast lines from fishing boats above,
bait hooks for grandchildren seated alongside,
share stories of childhood memories
and tales of Danville's glory days.

Congeniality

Does Cormorant regret sleeping in
the day Creator visited the river valley,
bestowing avian gifts to early-rising relatives?

No, he frets not over Eagle's strength,
Mallard's waterproof plumage,
or Loon's remarkable song.

He shows no envy of Heron's grace,
Pelican's aeronautic precision,
even Frigatebird's mating display.

Cormorant wraps webbed feet around silvered perch,
spreads lackluster wings aside gangly frame
to air-dry soggy post-swim feathers.

Head held high, he thanks Creator for friendship
and grunts in unabashed conversation
with his blue-eyed, flame-faced besties.

Boat Ramp Rescue

Faint plaintive cries pull me close,
fear-filled emerald eyes search mine.
Tiny Yoda face warily tests,
then gobbles my salmon lunch.

White mittens, boots and bib
nestle amidst black velvet fur,
our grass-lined cookpot her seat
to a day of river adventure.

Barely audible snores drift from below.
She wakes, explores, tickles my legs,
climbs to my lap, watches the river swirl past.
A mere fifteen miles capture my heart.

Kayak kitten becomes marina princess,
held, cuddled, fed, adored by all,
finds her forever home on solid ground.
My joy tempered only by heartache.

Gators and Snakes

Thanks for telling me, friend,
about the gator you saw, just yesterday,
as long as our boat and at least as wide…
and about the thirteen-footer you released
at this very boat ramp just last spring.

Maybe I *am* better off knowing
water moccasins hang out in clumps
of shoreside grass and bask on sunny paths…
that you've seen rattlers swim across the river,
heads and maraca tails both held high.

I might not have known, otherwise,
to scan muddy banks for alligator slides,
question every suspicious twig…
anxiously plan for quick getaways
at rest stops along our way.

But I rather enjoyed paddling without concern
that my next stroke might be my demise…
when my biggest worries were donating blood
to leeches and screaming in surprise
at jumping Asian carp.

River Sculptor

Painstakingly etched of soil and stone,
kinetic works of art evolve along the shore,
from tools of water and wind
at the river sculptor's hand.

Stalwart trunks stretch skyward,
current-carved roots reach below,
grasping for washed-away earth,
awaiting gravity's insistent call.

Layers of shale—gray, mocha and cream—
line the water's edge, sliced by evergreen roots
into scrumptious squares of tiramisu,
scattered crumbs smoothed to round pebbles.

Sand, silt and stone carved from one bend,
the sculptor deposits at another,
new growth on a new path,
ever-changing landscape of design.

Stuck on a Stump

How did we get here, high and dry,
in the middle of a stump field bay?
Submerged tree trunk under our hull,
looks like we're here to stay.

Attempts to jiggle from the errant perch,
only serve to wedge us higher.
I'm sure I spot gators lurking about.
This predicament does seem dire.

Is that a house at the crest of the hill?
Should we wave and scream for aid?
I'm not even sure I want to be found,
embarrassed more than afraid.

Stumps all around sprout blossoms
like flowerpots of sundry sizes.
This isn't such a terrible place
to wait 'til the water rises.

Paddle Partner

When you asked for my hand and I said, "I do,"
I never guessed what was in store:
tent-dwelling, paddling, rehydrated meals,
two thousand miles, even more.

We had our share of better or worse:
stunning vistas, rough waves and foul weather.
Camped on islands of sand under starlit skies,
faced wet exits and joint aches together.

Of everyone here on God's green earth
I'd want twenty-four/seven with me,
through bugs, ibuprofen and calamine lotion,
You're the only one it would be.

Journey's End

Riverbanks, our summer companions and guides,
usher us to the gulf, then fall away without direction,
freedom to wander, no course set but our own.

River's end transforms to saltwater sea.
Droplets of paddle spray send concentric ripples
toward the Florida coast and beaches of Cozumel,
adventures reserved for another time.

With wide sweeping turn, we head toward shore.
Beams of golden light stream from above,
cast an opalescent glow across the calm evening sea.

Barb Geiger, now retired from her teaching career, lives and writes in Waukesha, Wisconsin. Her first book, *Paddle for a Purpose* (eLectio Publishing, 2018), received the 2019 First Place Pencraft Award in the category of memoir. Barb's poems have been published in anthologies by Pure Slush Books and in several Wisconsin Fellowship of Poets' calendars. *Mississippi Meanderings* (Finishing Line Press) is her first poetry chapbook.

Barb is a member of the Authors Guild and the Wisconsin Fellowship of Poets. She participates in writing workshops at AllWriters' Workplace & Workshop and credits her success as an author to the dedicated staff and supportive writing community she enjoys there.

Barb and her husband, Gene, share a love of nature and enjoy watching birds at their feeders, deer that visit from the nearby nature conservancy, and the pair of mallard ducks that return every spring. Barb also enjoys volunteering, spending time with friends and family, and being outside on bikes and boats.

You can see photos and an interactive map of Barb and Gene's Mississippi River travels at www.paddleforapurpose.net. Photos accompanying the poems in Mississippi Meanderings and more about Barb's writing can be found on her author website at *www.barbgeiger.com*.

www.ingramcontent.com/pod-product-compliance
Lightning Source LLC
Chambersburg PA
CBHW020220090426
42734CB00008B/1155